First Facts®

Long Ago and Today

COMMUNICATION
LONG AGO and TODAY

by Lindsy O'Brien

Consultant:
Daniel Zielske
Professor of Anthropology
South Central College
North Mankato, Minnesota

CAPSTONE PRESS
a capstone imprint

First Facts are published by Capstone Press,
1710 Roe Crest Drive, North Mankato, Minnesota 56003
www.capstonepub.com

Library of Congress Cataloging-in-Publication Data
Lindsy O'Brien
Communication long ago and today / Lindsy O'Brien.
pages cm.—(Long ago and today)
Includes bibliographical references and index.
ISBN 978-1-4914-0295-5 (library binding)
ISBN 978-1-4914-0303-7 (paperback)
ISBN 978-1-4914-0299-3 (eBook PDF)
Communication—History—Juveline literature. Communication—Juveline. I. Title.
P91.2 .O37 2015
302.209   2013050323

Editorial Credits
Nate LeBoutillier, editor; Juliette Peters, designer; Eric Gohl, media researcher; Tori Abraham, production specialist

Photo Credits
Bridgeman Art Library: © Look and Learn/Private Collection, 20; Capstone Studio: Karon Dubke, 21; Library of Congress: 9, 11, 13; Newscom: Everett Collection, 15, Mirrorpix/NCJ, 17; Shutterstock: Adrio Communications Ltd, 1 (left), Blend Images, 5, cobalt88, 1 (right), Everett Collection, cover (top), Nestor Noci, 7, ra2studio, cover (bottom), 18, Toria, background

Printed in the United States of America in North Mankato, Minnesota
032014   008087CGF14

TABLE OF CONTENTS

COMMUNICATION IN OUR WORLD

People love to find new ways to communicate. Long ago people used bits of clay to pass on news and keep track of information. They passed messages through facial expressions and by making shapes with their hands. Today tools like **computers** send messages across the world. Communication has changed a lot over time.

● ●

computer—an electronic machine used to store and manage information and do calculations

MAKING A MARK:
ANCIENT TIMES
30,000 BC–AD 1000

Early people liked to draw. They wrote on cave walls and pots. They drew animals and people. They also painted **hieroglyphics**. The first letters were made 5,000 years ago. They came from China and Italy. Today people find stones carved with these old letters.

• •

hieroglyphics—pictures used by early people to communicate

ancient Egyptian carvings in stone

WORDS ON A PAGE:
LATE MIDDLE AGES
1000-1775

People started making paper in Europe around 1200. Early books were copied by hand. They cost a lot of money. Johann Gutenberg invented the printing press in 1446. This machine copied typed pages quickly. Some kids began to use books as families could keep books in their homes.

Johann Gutenberg
inspecting his work

MOVING MESSAGES:
THE AGE OF REVOLUTION
1775-1850

People first moved mail by hand around 1775. The Pony Express began in the United States in 1860. Riders on horseback delivered mail across the country. People later used boats, trains, and planes. Long ago it took weeks to get mail over oceans. Now it takes just a few days with planes.

Pony Express rider

The Rise of the Telephone and the Telegraph:
THE TURN OF THE 20TH CENTURY
1850-1910

Telephones were invented in the late 1800s. They let voices travel by wires. People could call a doctor, the police, or family members. Whole streets had just one phone number at first. The phone rang in all houses on the "party line."

FACT:
The **telegraph** came out in the mid-1800s. It used a code called Morse Code. "S.O.S." was the code for "help."

telegraph—a machine that uses electrical signals to send messages over long distances

man using an early telephone

PHILO'S FANCY:
THE TELECOMMUNICATION AGE
1910-1970

In the early 1900s, many people began to buy radios for their homes. Both adults and kids listened to radio shows for fun. They also listened for news of wars and other important events. In 1921 14-year-old Philo T. Farnsworth had an idea. His idea used a spot of light. The light made pictures that moved. This led to the first TVs.

FACT:
Today many TVs use **satellites.** Information on Earth is sent to satellites in space. Those signals are sent back to TVs all over the world.

teacher and students
watching TV in 1954

satellite—a spacecraft that circles the
Earth to gather and send information

COMPUTERS:
THE INFORMATION AGE
1970-PRESENT

Early computers were as big as entire rooms. Smaller home computers were new in the 1970s. The **Internet** became popular in the 1990s. Cell phones soon appeared too. People now communicate every day using computers and **smartphones**. They use smartphones for calls, sending text messages and e-mails, to get information, and for fun.

• •

Internet—a system that connects computers all over the world

smartphone—a phone that also functions as a computer

schoolchildren using
a computer in 1983

COMMUNICATION
IN THE FUTURE

Computers may one day be even tinier than they are today. They could be as small as the head of a pin. New computers already scan eyes and show people's names and information using these scans. People may even use electric pulses in their brains to communicate. The world changes fast. We can only guess how people will communicate in the future.

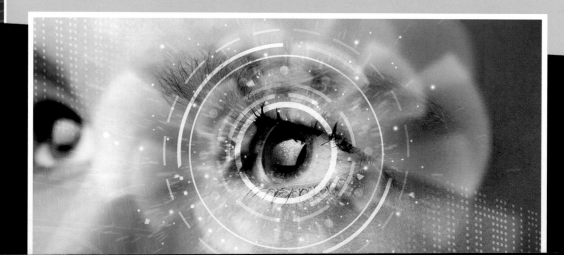

TIMELINE

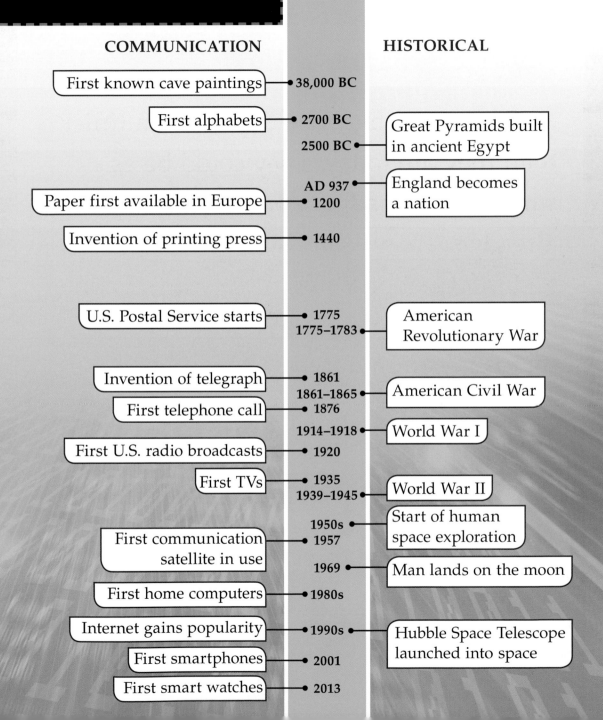

COMMUNICATION

HISTORICAL

First known cave paintings — 38,000 BC

First alphabets — 2700 BC

2500 BC — Great Pyramids built in ancient Egypt

AD 937 — England becomes a nation

Paper first available in Europe — 1200

Invention of printing press — 1440

U.S. Postal Service starts — 1775

1775–1783 — American Revolutionary War

Invention of telegraph — 1861

1861–1865 — American Civil War

First telephone call — 1876

1914–1918 — World War I

First U.S. radio broadcasts — 1920

First TVs — 1935

1939–1945 — World War II

1950s — Start of human space exploration

First communication satellite in use — 1957

1969 — Man lands on the moon

First home computers — 1980s

Internet gains popularity — 1990s — Hubble Space Telescope launched into space

First smartphones — 2001

First smart watches — 2013

History's Most Famous Messenger

A Greek man named Pheidippides (fye-DIP-id-ees) once carried an important message. He ran more than 25 miles (40 kilometers) to Athens from the city of Marathon. His job was to share the news that the Greek army had won an important battle. He was so tired when he got to Marathon that he fell down and died. People now run 26.2-mile (42.2-kilometer) races called marathons in his honor.

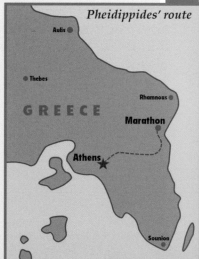

Pheidippides' route

Hands On:
MAKE AN ALUMINUM CAN TELEPHONE

What You Need:
2 empty aluminum cans
   with top lids removed
10 feet (3 meters) of string
small nail
hammer
a friend
an adult

What You Do:
1. Take the open end of one can. Place it on a table or on the floor. Ask an adult to use the hammer and nail to make a hole in the bottom of the can. Repeat this with the other can.
2. Thread one end of the string through one hole. Make a knot in the string on the inside of the can. Repeat with the other can and the other end of the string. The cans should be connected.

3. Hold one can. Give the other to your friend. Walk away from each other until the string is tight. Speak into the open end of one can. Your friend should listen to the open end of the other can. Then switch roles.

Can you hear your friend? Does the sound change with a longer string? Try to talk from down a long hall or between rooms. Can you still hear each other?

GLOSSARY

computer (kuhm-PYOO-tur)—an electronic machine used to store and manage information and do calculations

hieroglyphics (hiy-ro-GLIF-iks)—pictures used by early people to communicate

Internet (IN-tur-net)—a system that connects computers all over the world

satellite (SAT-uh-lite)—a spacecraft that circles the Earth to gather and send information

smartphone (SMART-fone)—a phone that uses the Internet and acts like a tiny computer

telegraph (TEL-uh-graf)—a machine that uses electrical signals to send messages over long distances

READ MORE

Gregory, Jillian. *Making Secret Codes.* Making and Breaking Codes. Mankato, Minn.: Capstone Press, 2011.

Lin, Yoming S. *Alexander Graham Bell and the Telephone.* Inventions and Discovery. New York: Powerkids Press, 2012.

Rand, Casey. *Communication.* The Science Behind. Chicago: Raintree, 2012.

INTERNET SITES

FactHound offers a safe, fun way to find Internet sites related to this book. All of the sites on FactHound have been researched by our staff.

Here's all you do:

Visit *www.facthound.com*

Type in this code: 9781491402955

Check out projects, games and lots more at
www.capstonekids.com

CRITICAL THINKING
USING THE COMMON CORE

1. At one time, books were printed by hand. How did the printing press change the way knowledge was communicated? (Key Ideas and Details)

2. Look at the photograph on p. 17 and then read the text on p. 16. In what ways have computers changed since that photo was taken? (Craft and Structure)

INDEX